A WRITER'S GUIDE

TO
USING
EIGHT METHODS
OF
TRANSITION

Dan —
Much aloha ... Vic
4-27-93

Victor C. Pellegrino

MAUI ARTHOUGHTS COMPANY
P.O. Box 967
Wailuku, HI, USA 96793-0967

Pellegrino, Victor C.
A Writer's Guide to Using Eight Methods of Transition

International Standard Book Number: 0-945045-03-4
Library of Congress Catalog Card Number: 93-77683

A short guide of the eight methods of transition; helps writers
connect sentences and paragraphs to create a smooth flow of
ideas in order to communicate clearly and effectively. This book
is a companion text for *A Writer's Guide to Transitional Words
and Expressions*.

Published
by

MAUI ARTHOUGHTS COMPANY
P.O. Box 967
Wailuku, HI, USA 96793-0967
Phone/FAX (808) 244-0156

DEDICATION

To my wife

Wallette Pualani Lyn-fah

To my children

Shelley Jeanne Laʻelaʻeokala Lyn-oi
Angela Terese Mahinamalamalama Mei-lyn
Christopher Joseph Bailey Hoku-ao Wu-wei

To my parents

Albert and Adeline Pellegrino

CONTENTS

PREFACE

A Writer's Guide to Using Eight Methods of Transition is designed as a complementary text for *A Writer's Guide to Transitional Words and Expressions*. Writers who use both books regularly will learn how to embed a greater variety of transition in their writing and create more effective prose. In addition, they will realize that this variety will reduce redundancies, add liveliness, and provide the kind of connections in writing that make readers able to follow their ideas--from point to point, from paragraph to paragraph, and from beginning to end.

This text identifies eight methods of transition: *Transitional Words and Expressions, Pronoun Reference, Repeating Key Words, Word Substitution, Repeating Key Phrases or Clauses, Beginning-of-Paragraph Transition, End-of-Paragraph Transition, and the Transitional Paragraph.* Each method is explained clearly and examples are provided for writers to study and emulate.

The first chapter, *Transitional Words and Expressions*, includes examples and explanations of each of the fifteen sections of *A Writer's Guide to Transitional Words and Expressions*. Subsections for this chapter are numbered from 1-A to 15-A and follow in the same order as the sections in *A Writer's Guide to Transitional Words and Expressions (see p. 52-53).*

One chapter of the text, *Pronoun Reference,* is intended to be especially comprehensive. This is because using pronouns correctly and effectively is a problem for many writers. This section includes a helpful listing of all seven categories of pronouns. To help writers, each listing has accompanying explanations and examples of correct usage.

Another important chapter is *Repeating Key Phrases or Clauses*. This chapter provides examples of parallel structure to help writers with difficulties they encounter when trying to keep ideas in a sentence or a series of sentences similar in construction. Writers should realize that parallelism, although a very important part of clear writing, is only one of many ways to repeat phrases or clauses.

A Writer's Guide to Using Eight Methods of Transition and *A Writer's Guide to Transitional Words and Expressions* are effective reference tools for writers of all ages, backgrounds, and jobs. Writers who use these two resources regularly are guaranteed to develop effective coherence. Indeed, their readers will be more than satisfied when they receive writing that is clear and connected.

A Writer's Guide
to
Using
Eight Methods
of
Transition

A WRITER'S GUIDE
TO USING
EIGHT METHODS OF TRANSITION

To use transition effectively, you will need to study, learn, and practice different transitional techniques. Then your writing will become clear and coherent. To that end, this brief guide includes eight useful methods of achieving effective transition and examples that will help you understand how to make important connections in writing. These eight methods are included because the key to lively writing is variety; therefore, you should aim to use as many different kinds of transition as possible. Finally, practice using all eight methods *consciously*. In a short time, you will be using them *naturally* to create the kind of clear and effective communication readers expect.

TRANSITIONAL WORDS
AND
EXPRESSIONS

Use *transitional words and expressions* as signal words to tell your readers that you are moving from one point to the next. When you connect your sentences and paragraphs in this way, you help readers see relationships between points rather than create confusion with fragmented ideas. Selecting transitional words and expressions should not be a result of guesswork. Look through the fifteen sections of *A Writer's Guide to Transitional Words and Expressions* (see *Preface*, pp. 7-8) to determine the general meaning you wish to convey. Then decide which section best suits what you are trying to communicate.

For example, if you were to convey your dissatisfaction through a letter of complaint about a defective product, you could explain *how* it malfunctioned by using *sequence* entries such as *first, later, finally, etc.* On the other hand, if you wished to explain *what* part broke, you could use *spatial* entries such as *inside, next to, below, etc.* In contrast to these two approaches, if you wanted to develop your points by showing *increasing importance,* you could use the *emphasize-intensify* entries such as *especially, more importantly, furthermore, and most important of all.* Using these connecting words and phrases in your letter will create interrelationships that enable the reader to achieve a clearer understanding of your complaint.

Examine the following paragraphs. Note how the absence of transitional words and expressions in the first example creates fragmented and staccato-like sentences, whereas the addition of transitional words and expressions in the second example creates clear connections and interrelationships that help the reader move from point to point easily.

POOR

Daniel and I have several things in common that have strengthened our relationship. We are Asian Americans. Both of us were born of middle class parents in San Francisco and lived on the same block on the East side. We got to know each other early in our lives. A commonality is our age. We have shared similar interests over the years we have known each other. Both of us enjoyed taking piano lessons. We each worked summers at Burger King to help our parents reduce the expenses for us to

12

attend the University of Colorado, where we both majored in art. What has bonded us together is our mutual respect for each other. We hold diverse opinions, represent different political and religious beliefs, and lead unique life-styles. We have remained close to each other even to this day--our twentieth class reunion.

BETTER

Daniel and I have several things in common that have strengthened our relationship. *First of all*, we are Asian Americans. Both of us were born of middle class parents in San Francisco and lived on the same block on the East side. *As a result*, we got to know each other early in our lives. *Another* commonality is our age. *In fact*, we have shared similar interests over the years we have known each other. Both of us enjoyed taking piano lessons. *In addition*, we each worked summers at Burger King to help our parents reduce the expenses for us to attend the University of Colorado, where we both majored in art. *The most significant thing* that has bonded us together is our mutual respect for each other. *Certainly* we hold diverse opinions, represent different political and religious beliefs, and lead unique lifestyles; we have, *nonetheless*, remained close to each other even to this day--our twentieth class reunion.

1 - A

TO INDICATE TIME ORDER

Use time order transitional words and expressions to connect ideas or information in a framework that indicates a chronological passage of time. Time order transitions are divided into three categories: past, present and future. To indicate movement of time, use these transitions in a series of sentences, or embed them in paragraphs for larger pieces of writing, such as letters, reports, or essays.

EXAMPLE

There were times *in the past* when I thought that living in a large city would be more dangerous than living in a rural area. *Not long ago* my job transfer forced me to relocate to Chicago. *Initially*, my *earlier* notion proved correct. My new neighborhood was clearly unsafe. *All the while* I lived there, I had to practice being "street smart." It wasn't *until later* in the year that I began to feel safe. *Now* I realize that although living in the city might not be completely safe, I am more comfortable living there than I had thought.

2 - A

TO INDICATE HOW OR WHEN SOMETHING OCCURS IN TIME

Use transitional words and expressions to indicate how or when something occurs in time not only to connect a number of points, but also to make ideas more exacting. Things that occur in time will mean something quite different if, for example, *always* were to be used in place of *sometimes*, or *intermittently* were to be used in place of *all of the time*. Because good writing demands concreteness, using how or when transitions helps writers avoid confusion, ambiguity, and vagueness.

EXAMPLE

Frequently well-meaning clients tend to forget making payments to small vendors. Our company *promptly* calls these clients *as soon as* the thirty-day grace period ends. As a result, *rarely* do we experience a default on payment, and *without exception* our customers are apologetic *as long as* we are direct and polite on the phone.

3 - A

TO INDICATE SEQUENCE

Use transitional words and expressions to indicate a sequence of events. In that way, points that follow one another will be connected logically. Whether a police officer writes an accident report, an attorney writes a statement of demand, a business person writes a letter, or a student writes a story, sequential transition effectively signals the reader that events occur from an initial to a final stage. Sequential transition is an effective technique for anyone writing "how to" explanations, from simple recipes to complex scientific processes for a textbook. When writing information in time sequence, writers should make sure no step or event is omitted; otherwise the reader may become confused.

EXAMPLE

To prepare a letter of complaint in climactic sequence about a defective product, a writer should follow a few simple steps. *To begin with*, explain the problem clearly. *Following that* use transition to emphasize or intensify, such as "of major concern" or "even more important" to explain the effects of the problem. Begin the *next* paragraph with "most important of all" or "without question" to request a refund, a repair or a replacement of the product. *Last of all*, make sure to include copies of the proof of purchase and product guarantee. You can be sure that writing a clear, sequential letter will, *in the end*, lead to positive results.

4-A

TO REPEAT

All writers have their favorite transitional entries for repeating. In fact, because they are "favorites," they are frequently overused and create redundancies. Because the key to good writing is variety, particularly within a lengthy letter, essay, or report, embed different transitional words and phrases for purposes of repetition. A second point about repetition is that if used appropriately, it will strengthen a viewpoint or idea. Finally, use several of the words and expressions to culminate an idea in a paragraph or to conclude a longer piece of writing. For example, a paragraph can culminate with "in view of" or a longer piece of writing can conclude with "to reconsider" or "to summarize."

EXAMPLE

Most wars are founded on differences--sometimes, ironically, differences based on religion or ethnic origin. For example, conflicts in India originated among Hindus, Moslems, and Sikhs. *Likewise,* war in China erupted between the Hans and Mongolians. *In other words,* the initial causes of war are simply less "political" than we are led to believe.

5 - A

TO PROVIDE AN EXAMPLE

One of the best ways to explain is by using examples. An example must always be a clear representation of a larger body of information. To illustrate, explain the layout of a business letter by choosing a single example to describe the left block form; to explain more clearly, select multiple examples, first by describing the left block form and then by describing the indented form. These multiple examples can be extended by comparing and contrasting the two forms. There are numerous ways to provide examples, but in any explanation avoid repeating "pet" transitions, most frequently the overused "for example" and "for instance," in order to avoid redundancies.

EXAMPLE

Choosing the correct format for a business letter is not only controversial among sticklers of form, but also it is an important consideration because of the results people desire. *By way of illustration,* one person wrote a letter of complaint using the block form while another wrote using the indented form. The first writer was denied her request, yet the second writer received a refund. *In this instance*, what many proponents of the indented form believe proved correct: the "white space" created by indenting suggests a visually "friendlier tone," thereby lending itself to a more favorable response from the recipient. *To put it another way,* who ever argued that form is unimportant?

6 - A

TO CONCEDE

Most writers are reluctant to concede, particularly because they think that doing so smacks of defeat. To the contrary, frequently agreeing, and more specifically admitting, can lead to winning as well. For example, when using "although this may be true," the concession can be followed by "of course," or when using "to comply with," the transition initiates a tone of willingness and cooperation. Admittedly, weigh any concessions before locking them in black and white, but also realize that making a concession does not always denote losing.

EXAMPLE (Showing concession of writer)

Drinking alcohol excessively is clearly dangerous to oneself and to others. It is known that people who drink too much reduce their life span; in addition to that, women who drink during pregnancy affect their fetuses adversely. Most important of all, some people who drive drunk kill innocent bystanders. Nonetheless, people still continue to drink excessively and without concern for themselves or others. *Although this may be true*, I contend that there is nothing wrong with imbibing "socially" as long as one does so moderately. *To admit the truth*, I am this kind of drinker, and it just makes good, common sense to belong to this latter group of imbibers as opposed to drinking excessively.

EXAMPLE (Showing concession in content)

The Third International Conference turned out to be more positive than the confrontation everyone had expected;

instead of arguing, high ranking officials worked in a spirit of cooperation. *To comply with* the new arms reduction agreement, South Korean representatives attempted *to accommodate* North Korea's "Twelve Demands" involving four decades of border disputes. *At the same time*, North Korean delegates decided *to reconcile* centuries-old ethnic differences with South Korea by releasing political prisoners. For both sides, *acquiescing* resulted in triumph.

7 - A

TO CONCLUDE
OR
TO SUMMARIZE

It is important to signal readers as they near the end of a piece of writing. For short pieces, use concluding transition; for longer pieces, such as reports or chapter-length material, use summarizing transition. A concluding transition ends the writing process with three or four good sentences; a good way to end is to return to the introduction, find the main idea, and use it as a springboard to write the conclusion. In this way, the conclusion will reinforce the main idea and create composition unity.

On the other hand, a summarizing transition provides an abbreviated repetition of the main ideas for a longer piece of writing. If necessary, it may be more than one paragraph in length, depending on the complexity of ideas. Its purpose is not only to refresh the reader by presenting the main points, but also to strengthen or emphasize the main ideas. Last of all, never use summarizing transition for short pieces because it insults the reader; in contrast, avoid drawing short conclusions for lengthy pieces that deserve transitional depth because, in the end, a reader welcomes a summary--which acts as a form of repetition that strengthens and draws attention to important points.

EXAMPLE   (Conclusion for a main idea that focuses on the view that more people should take advantage of herbal medicines)

Consequently, instead of going to a pharmacy for a bottle of anti-diarrheal medicine, a box of blood pressure tablets, or a tube of salve for burns, look for remedies in your own back yard such as a few tiny leaves from the guava tree, a bunch of lemon grass, or a stem from an aloe plant. The rewards will be "eternal."

EXAMPLE (Summary for a main idea that focuses on the view that more people should take advantage of herbal medicines)

To summarize, readers need only take note that herbs found in their own back yard are effective remedies for common problems such as diarrhea, high blood pressure, and burns. The tiny leaves at the tips of the guava tree will unfailingly stop diarrhea; lemon grass boiled in water and removed will result in an effective drink to combat high blood pressure; and the gluey liquid from the aloe plant will act as a soothing, natural salve for common household burns. Not only are these herbal remedies free, but also they are nature's way of taking care of us in modern times without having to resort to chemically processed "foreign" substances. In the end, those who take full advantage of herbal medicines will save money, improve health, and live longer.

8 - A

TO ADD A POINT

Many writers use the same transitional word or expression over and over without realizing that there are many other choices of transition available to create a variety of sequences. First, although some of the add-a-point transitions do just that--add a point--others "add" more uniquely. For example, "equally important" gives balance to ideas and allows for points to be compared; "above all" stresses the development of ideas from the least to the most important; "least of all" suggests the lack of importance of a final point in a series.

To write a sequential paragraph or a longer sequential piece such as an essay, choose "first, next, then, after that, and finally" to show transitional addition in time order; or choose "initially, in the second place, subsequently, to add to that, and most of all" to show addition in climactic order. Thus, use add-a-point transition not only to add a single point, but also to structure multiple points for lengthier pieces of writing such as letters, reports, essays, or chapters in a book.

EXAMPLE

There are several plans of action that your community group can follow. *First of all,* begin an awareness campaign using the media; *following that,* set up booths at key shopping centers to attract and enlist new volunteers; *finally,* demonstrate a commitment for change by beginning and supporting a political action campaign. *As a result,* your dream of reducing crime will begin to shape itself into reality.

9 - A

TO COMPARE

Use transitional words and expressions to compare. Showing likenesses will make writing crisper and more concrete. To say that something has "a strong resemblance" to something else or that something "parallels" something else allows the reader to make associations more precisely. In addition, use comparative transition to structure ideas within paragraphs and essays. Every time a writer adds a comparison, the main idea becomes clearer and clearer.

EXAMPLE

The PC and MAC are *similar* in several ways, even though users of either computer would rather die than admit even a small *resemblance*. Both machines will run graphics *in much the same way*. Each employs a mouse and a graphical interface or windows-like environment *in a similar fashion* to run programs such as PageMaker or Microsoft Word. The final *likeness* is that both the PC and the MAC incorporate technology that allows them to "talk" to each other. In just a few more years, the PC and MAC will become even more *alike*, and users will be less adamant about the unique qualities of their computers.

10 - A

TO CONTRAST

Use transitional words and expressions to contrast objects, ideas or points of view to make writing more exacting. To say that something "has a striking difference" to something else or that something "is diametrically opposed" to something else allows the reader to see differences more precisely. In addition, use contrasting transition to structure ideas within paragraphs and essays. Every time a writer adds contrast, the main idea becomes clearer and clearer.

EXAMPLE

Although one might classify both Chinese and Japanese people together because they are Asians, they are *dissimilar* in many ways. First of all, Chinese are independent, but Japanese are group-oriented. The Chinese developed Taoism, the tea ceremony and lacquerware, *but* the Japanese, *in contrast* to the Chinese, molded Taoism into Zen, restructured the tea ceremony into an exacting ritual, and improved lacquerware to a state of near perfection. *The most striking differences* between the two Asian neighbors are their economies and governments. China is still considered a "third world" nation that embraces communistic economic theory, and its government is largely a dictatorship; Japan, *on the other hand*, has adopted capitalism and a democratic form of government. Thus, if one were to continue *contrasting* the Chinese and Japanese, their *differences* would far outweigh their similarities.

11 - A

TO INDICATE CAUSE AND EFFECT

Developing logical cause and effect relationships depends on a writer's ability to use transition. Differences in meaning can be generated by changing one transitional word or phrase, so careful diction is essential. It is important to realize that the cause-effect relationship is more realistically a cause-effect-cause-effect, etc. string. Whether writing about a series of misfortunes in a personal essay or stating data in objective reports, show clear relationships and draw accurate and logical conclusions.

The most obvious cause and effect writing occurs when making a transition for the conclusion. As a note of caution, when using cause and effect transition for conclusions, avoid what is commonly called a non sequitur (the conclusion does not follow logically from the premises), and the inductive leap (the conclusion becomes a hasty generalization because information is left out of the argument; this is commonly known as "jumping to conclusions").

EXAMPLE

Last month two youths robbed a man in an alley near Sixth Avenue and Maple Street. Just two weeks ago, neighbors witnessed two young drug dealers in the same area who were exchanging cash for crack. Last night, rival gangs clashed in the same alley and one youth was stabbed. *Therefore,* the Graven

Lake County Police Department launched a special twenty-four hour surveillance of the area in order to curtail further criminal activity and to ensure the safety of its citizens.

12 - A

TO DIVIDE
OR
TO CLASSIFY

Using transition that divides is basic to the writing process, particularly since writers very frequently explain by beginning with a subject and then dividing it into parts. These parts, or paragraphs, are a way of "taking apart" the whole subject and presenting it in single ideas. As the reader moves through a piece of writing paragraph by paragraph, the main idea becomes clearer and clearer. This method of writing is called enumeration or, more commonly, naming major topics.

Using transition to classify is another way of presenting ideas. When classifying, several subjects are placed into one class or category. For example, folk, rock, jazz, reggae, and classical fall into musical categories; or more specifically, Bach, Beethoven, and Brahms fall into the classical music category. Visually, the process of dividing resembles an inverted tree, while the process of classification looks like the tree itself.

EXAMPLE (Division)

World literature courses at most colleges in the United States emphasize western cultures and include very few works, if any, from Eastern cultures. The *elements* of Eastern literature are in many ways just as important as the *divisions* in Western literature. One cannot ignore India, any more than Greece, *for example,* when comparing epics such as The Mahabharata and The Ramayana to The Iliad and The Odyssey. *Another example* is the novel. Indian writers such as Markandaya and Banerji have produced novels that compare equally to writers in Western cultures, such as Cather and Faulkner. Thus, to preface literature courses with the word ''world,'' teachers must integrate literary works from both hemispheres.

EXAMPLE (Classification)

India, China, and Japan are three major Eastern cultures that have given the world important writers. Markandaya and Banerji can be grouped with the *first* country; Lao-tzu and Pa Chin can be classified with *the second* country; and Basho and Kawabata can be categorized with the *last* country.

13 - A

TO INDICATE SPATIAL ARRANGEMENT

Spatial transition is used when dealing with anything that takes up space or has to do with space. Whether writing an engineering report, directions for a travel book, or a description of an automobile accident for a police report, spatial transitional words and expressions play a key role in developing accuracy, clarity, and understanding. In the following example, imagine how lost the reader would become if the spatial transition were omitted.

EXAMPLE

Getting to McDonald's is easy. First go *straight ahead* one block. Then turn *left* at the intersection to get on Bell Street. *In the distance* and *on the left* is Parker's Department Store. Go *down* Bell Street until you are *near* Parker's. McDonald's is located *behind* Parker's at *the base* of the hill.

14 - A

TO EMPHASIZE
OR
TO INTENSIFY

One of the most effective ways to develop an idea is to divide a subject into levels from the least important point to the most important point. For example, use transition to emphasize or intensify for letters of complaint, collection letters, reports to produce action, arguments to convince, or student progress and behavior reports, to name just a few. Climactic transition is also effective when organizing ideas for persuasive essays, proposals, requests, and other pieces of writing that are issue-oriented or argue for action.

EXAMPLE

Three important occurrences during President Bush's administration changed the way that people perceive the American armed forces. *First,* Desert Storm awakened the world to America's massive air power. *Even more important than that,* the Los Angeles riots following the Rodney King decision focused on the special role that army reservists play in restoring peace and order. *The most significant* occurrence involved America's presence in Somalia, where armed troops acted as a peace-keeping force, brought food to the starving, and supplied much needed health care to the suffering masses.

15 - A

TO CONNECT CLAUSES

There are many rules and variations of rules regarding connecting clauses, but a few standard ones are important to follow. Use coordinating conjunctions to connect main clauses in compound sentences; use correlative conjunctions in pairs with subjects or to connect main clauses in compound sentences; use subordinating conjunctions to introduce dependent clauses in complex sentences; use conjunctive adverbs in complete sentences; and use relative pronouns to form dependent clauses in complex sentences. For additional help on connecting clauses, refer to *A Writer's Guide to Transitional Words and Expressions* (see *Preface*, pp. 7-8.) Last of all, because there are many comma rules, use a recent manual of style to learn more about punctuation.

EXAMPLES

Coordinating Conjunctions

Football is an exciting sport to watch, *but* it is a dangerous sport to play. (Note the comma prior to the coordinating conjunction.)

Correlative Conjunctions

Not only is football an exciting sport to watch, *but also* it is a dangerous sport to play. (Note the comma prior to *but also*.)

Subordinating Conjunctions

Although football is an exciting sport to watch, it is a dangerous sport to play. (Note the comma setting off the subordinate clause from the main clause.)

Conjunctive Adverbs

Football is an exciting sport to watch; *however*, it is a dangerous sport to play. (Note the semicolon before the conjunctive adverb and the comma following it.)

Relative Pronouns

Whichever way you look at it, football is an exciting sport to watch but a dangerous sport to play. (Note the comma setting off the dependent clause from the main clause.)

2

PRONOUN REFERENCE

Use *pronoun reference* to show relationships and connections within a sentence, paragraph or essay. One of the gravest errors you can make with pronouns is not keeping them parallel to their antecedents (the nouns and pronouns to which they refer). If you unconsciously *shift* sentence structure so that the pronoun does not follow the general grammatical pattern that you have set up, you will confuse your reader. Below is a short paragraph that illustrates inaccurate pronoun reference. Following it is the corrected paragraph.

POOR

Sun and rain--it is what makes a rainbow. Whether they are children or adults, this temporary vision is what makes you realize the simple yet awe-inspiring beauty of nature.

BETTER

Sun and rain--*they* are what make a rainbow. Whether *we* are children or adults, the temporary vision of a rainbow is what makes *us* realize the simple yet awe-inspiring beauty of nature.

Using pronouns correctly requires study and practice. Learn what the different kinds of pronouns are and how they are used. To help you, read about the eight basic categories of pronouns that follow, and study the examples of how to use them.

PERSONAL PRONOUNS are used as substitutes for animate or inanimate things. These pronouns fall into three groups. Subjective pronouns are used as subjects: *I* have the dish. Objective pronouns are used as objects: Give the dish to *her*. Possessive pronouns are used to show ownership: *His* is older than *yours*.

SUBJECTIVE		*OBJECTIVE*		*POSSESSIVE*	
Singular	Plural	Singular	Plural	Singular	Plural
I	we	me	us	my, mine	our, ours
you	you	you	you	your, yours	your, yours
he, she	they	him, her	them	his, her	their
it		it		hers, its	theirs

DEMONSTRATIVE PRONOUNS (*this, these, that, those*) are used to point things out: *These* are my best paintings.

RELATIVE PRONOUNS (*who, whoever, whom, whomever, which, whichever, that, whose*) refer to objects or people: He is the person *who* killed the tiger. The bird *that* I want is similar to a small finch.

INTERROGATIVE PRONOUNS (all of the relative pronouns listed in the previous section except *that*) are used to ask a question and are followed by a verb. They are used in interrogative sentences: *Which* answer is correct? *Who* will attend the dance?

RECIPROCAL PRONOUNS (*each other and one another*) are used to show an interchange of action between two parties: Paul and his girlfriend, Jennifer, gave *each other* friendship rings on Valentine's Day.

INDEFINITE PRONOUNS are used when you cannot be exact, when you are unable to pin something down, and when you refer to nonspecific persons or things: *Each* of the officers served two terms. *Anything* is better than *nothing*. Indefinite pronouns are arranged in seven groups as follows:

one	some	any	anything
anyone	every	anybody	everything
each one	someone	somebody	something
no one	everyone	nobody	nothing
		everybody	

each	other	another
all	several	such
few	many	much
none	most	either
both		neither

REFLEXIVE AND INTENSIVE PRONOUNS are used to refer to a noun or pronoun: She found *herself* without money and with no place to go. Intensive pronouns are used to stress the preceding noun or pronoun: I plan to be there *myself*. Singular pronouns are (I) *myself*, (you) *yourself*, (he) *himself*, (she) herself, (the fox) *itself*. Use *oneself* (singular) for emphasis. One cures *oneself* by using herbal medicines. Plural pronouns are: (we) *ourselves*, (you) *yourselves*, and (they) *themselves*.

3

REPEAT KEY WORDS

Repeat key words, but not so frequently that you create redundancies or stifle and flatten your style of writing. When you repeat important words, you reinforce the point you are making as well as allow the reader to perceive a clearer relationship of ideas. Repetition also acts as a motif; that is, the words you repeat emphasize and tie your ideas into one image or theme. Use this technique in a short paragraph, as in the following example, or in a longer essay.

EXAMPLE

Reading poetry can be an especially moving experience, particularly when you choose the Romantics. *Ennui* is the least of your worries *when you read* Byron's ''When We *Two Parted.''* *Ennui* never occurs *when you read* Coleridge's ''Kubla Khan.'' Most of all, *ennui* is clearly out of the question *when you read* Keat's *"Ode On a Grecian Urn."*

4

WORD SUBSTITUTION

Use *word substitution* as a method of transition as well as a way to reduce redundancies. Employ it to add variety to your diction and to enliven your style of writing. The technique of word substitution is an effective one, but you must remember to choose words that are consistent in number (either singular or plural), that are not vague or obscure, and that are true derivatives or accurate synonyms. In addition, avoid using too many different word substitutions because they will create confusion instead of unity. Note how word substitution used in the second example reduces the redundancies contained in the first paragraph.

POOR

Senator John W. Baker has addressed the issue of arms reduction. Baker received support from both Republicans and Democrats. Baker traveled to Russia in order to reach an accord with Russian leaders about reducing the number of missiles that house atomic warheads. Moreover, Baker showed concern about humankind's inclination to destroy itself, and he took an important, though limited, first step in achieving greater arms reductions both in America and in Russia. Baker will be remembered for his efforts.

BETTER

Senator John W. Baker is one *leader* who has addressed the issue of arms reduction. Although a *Republican*, he received support from both Republicans and Democrats. *He* traveled to

Russia in order to reach an accord with Russian leaders about reducing the number of missiles that house atomic warheads. Moreover, *he* showed concern about humankind's inclination to destroy itself and took an important, though limited, first step in achieving greater arms reductions both in America and in Russia. *This senator* will be remembered as a *leader* for his efforts.

5

REPEAT KEY PHRASES
OR
CLAUSES

Repeat key phrases or clauses either within paragraphs or in the whole essay to achieve coherence as well as to emphasize or to strengthen a subject, viewpoint, or idea. This technique will help you to achieve consistency, to avoid shifts in thought, and to help your reader move from point to point and from paragraph to paragraph without misunderstanding your intent.

Repeating key phrases or clauses can help you write ideas in parallel structure (parallelism). This kind of repetition effectively sets up a pattern, movement, and sound that not only emphasizes the connection of ideas, but also creates a dramatic effect. In the following paragraph, notice how the elements in each sentence are parallel and balanced.

EXAMPLE

When countries with differing ideological viewpoints realize that war is not a solution, *peace is possible; when colonies* with political factions learn that confrontation is not prudent, *peace is viable;* most important of all, *when communities* with problems understand that diverse opinions are not without merit, *peace is achievable.*

6

BEGINNING-OF-PARAGRAPH TRANSITION

Use a *beginning-of-paragraph* sentence or two to repeat or echo the idea in the *previous* paragraph; then introduce your next point. This transitional technique allows you to shift from one point to the next and still make the change clear enough for your reader to follow.

EXAMPLE

Business executives are using *the airlines* more frequently than ever before. They realize that although air travel is expensive, the expense far outweighs *slow and inconvenient ground transportation.*

Avoiding slow and inconvenient ground transportation, however, is not the only objective of business executives who use the airlines; *they are also keenly interested in making more contacts with prospective clients abroad.*

7

END-OF-PARAGRAPH TRANSITION

Use an *end-of-paragraph* sentence or two to state or introduce briefly a new subject that you will discuss or address in the *following* paragraph. This transitional technique allows you to shift from one point to the next and still make the change clear enough for your reader to follow.

In the following end-of-paragraph example, note how the first paragraph moves from past to present as the subject of destruction is *introduced*. In the second paragraph, this *previously introduced* subject is expressed in a topic sentence.

EXAMPLE

The *advances in technology* during the Industrial Revolution were either attacked or praised by 19th century *writers. Today, writers express similar concerns, but with an ever-increasing awareness that our technological "know-how" forecasts our destruction.*

Advancements in technology--particularly in computer science--serve as a basis for modern writers to foresee our destruction. In one case, a writer explained that an airplane crashed because flaps were controlled not by manual means, but by a computer. In another case, an author described how a computer error nearly launched America's missiles toward Russia. More specifically . . .

8

THE TRANSITIONAL PARAGRAPH

If you are writing a lengthy essay and wish to shift from one idea to another, make use of the *transitional paragraph*. You can choose one of several approaches to develop the transitional paragraph: (1) Summarize and then introduce another point related to your thesis. This technique is useful when you are comparing and contrasting two points. (2) Shift your point of view or change the tone of your essay. This technique is useful when you shift from an individual to a collective view or when you change from a humorous tone to a serious one, or vice versa. (3) Use a rhetorical question. This technique is useful when you want to introduce a subject and then expand it. Regardless of the technique you choose, remember that the transitional paragraph is used both *to separate* and *to bridge* ideas so that the reader may follow your *intentional shift* from one point to another.

The suggestions above are a few of the variety of ways you can create a transitional paragraph. Read the example that follows. Note how the writer shifts from the subject of alcoholism to the subject of child abuse.

EXAMPLE

. . . about our concern for *victims of alcoholism.*

On the other hand, is it not true that we are failing to address very seriously the needs of victims of child abuse in the United States? Is it not also true that few support groups exist here

to help these sexually molested and physically battered children
solve their problems? Perhaps one answer lies in attracting
trained counselors and interested parents who will organize
help groups such as those currently available to drug abusers,
rape victims, and alcoholics.

This idea of forming help groups for *victims of child abuse*
is not new in other countries. In Australia, one help group,
founded last year, is called The Society to Help Save Abused
Children. In England, another help group formed this year. In the
United States, however, . . .

NOTES

NOTES

NOTES

NOTES

NOTES

NOTES

NOTES

WRITE, PHONE OR FAX
TO OBTAIN
COPIES OF . . .

A Writer's Guide to Transitional Words and Expressions
(ISBN 0-945045-02-6) $5.95 + $1.75 P&H
AND
A Writer's Guide to Using Eight Methods of Transition
(ISBN 0-945045-03-4) $5.95 + $1.75 P&H

When ordering by mail, make your check or money order payable to Maui Arthoughts Company and send it along with your name and address. Phone or FAX orders are welcome also, and book shipments will include your invoice. Inquire about discounts available to bookstores, educational institutions, and libraries as well as special quantity order discounts. All prices are subject to change without notice.

Maui Arthoughts Company
P.O. Box 967
Wailuku, HI, USA 96793-0967
Phone or FAX: (808) 244-0156

ORDER FORM...by Mail...Phone...FAX...

Mail Orders: Maui Arthoughts Company
P.O. Box 967
Wailuku, HI, USA 96793-0967

Phone/FAX Orders: (808) 244-0156

PLEASE SEND ME:

_____ copies of _A Writer's Guide to Transitional Words and Expressions_

_____ copies of _A Writer's Guide to Using Eight Methods of Transition_

_____ TOTAL copies X $5.95 per copy

_____ TOTAL copies X Quantity (15 or more) Discount Price:

     Retail Bookstores, less 40%, **$3.57**/copy

     College/Univ. Bookstores, less 25%, **$4.46**/copy

     Schools and Libraries, less 10%, **$5.35**/copy

HI Residents Add 4% Sales Tax

HI Bookstores, Schools & Libraries
     Add .5% Whsl. Tax

1st Class P&H (use chart below)

4th Class P&H (use chart below)

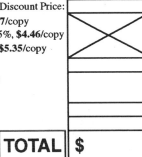

TOTAL	**$**

Name _____

Address _____

City _____ State_____ Zip_____

PAYMENT:
☐ Check/Money Order
☐ P.O. Number (Attach Purchase Order to order form)
☐ Bill me later

First Class (P&H)			Fourth Class Book Rate (P&H)		
# of Copies	Hawaii	All Other States	# of Copies	All States	* For 76 or more copies, please send my order:
1	1.75	1.75	1	1.50	☐ 1st Class
2-3	2.25	2.50	2-6	1.75	☐ 4th Class Book Rate
4-5	2.75	3.00	7-15	2.50	
6-15	4.00	5.00	16-20	3.00	
16-20	4.50	6.50	21-38	3.50	
21-28	5.00	7.50	39-47	4.50	Maui Arthoughts Co.
29-37	5.75	8.50	48-56	5.00	will bill you for P&H
38-47	6.50	9.50	57-66	5.50	charges.
48-57	7.75	10.50	67-75	6.50	
58-66	8.50	11.50	76 or more*		We can also ship and
67-75	10.00	13.50			bill you for _UPS_ if
76 or more*					requested.